TOYS "R" ME

Donald Gorbach

Copyright © 2017 by Donald Gorbach

All rights reserved.

ISBN-10 1979981728
ISBN-13 978-1979981729

"IT USUALLY TAKES TWO PEOPLE A LITTLE WHILE TO LEARN WHERE THE FUNNY BUTTONS ARE…"

— MATT LAUER

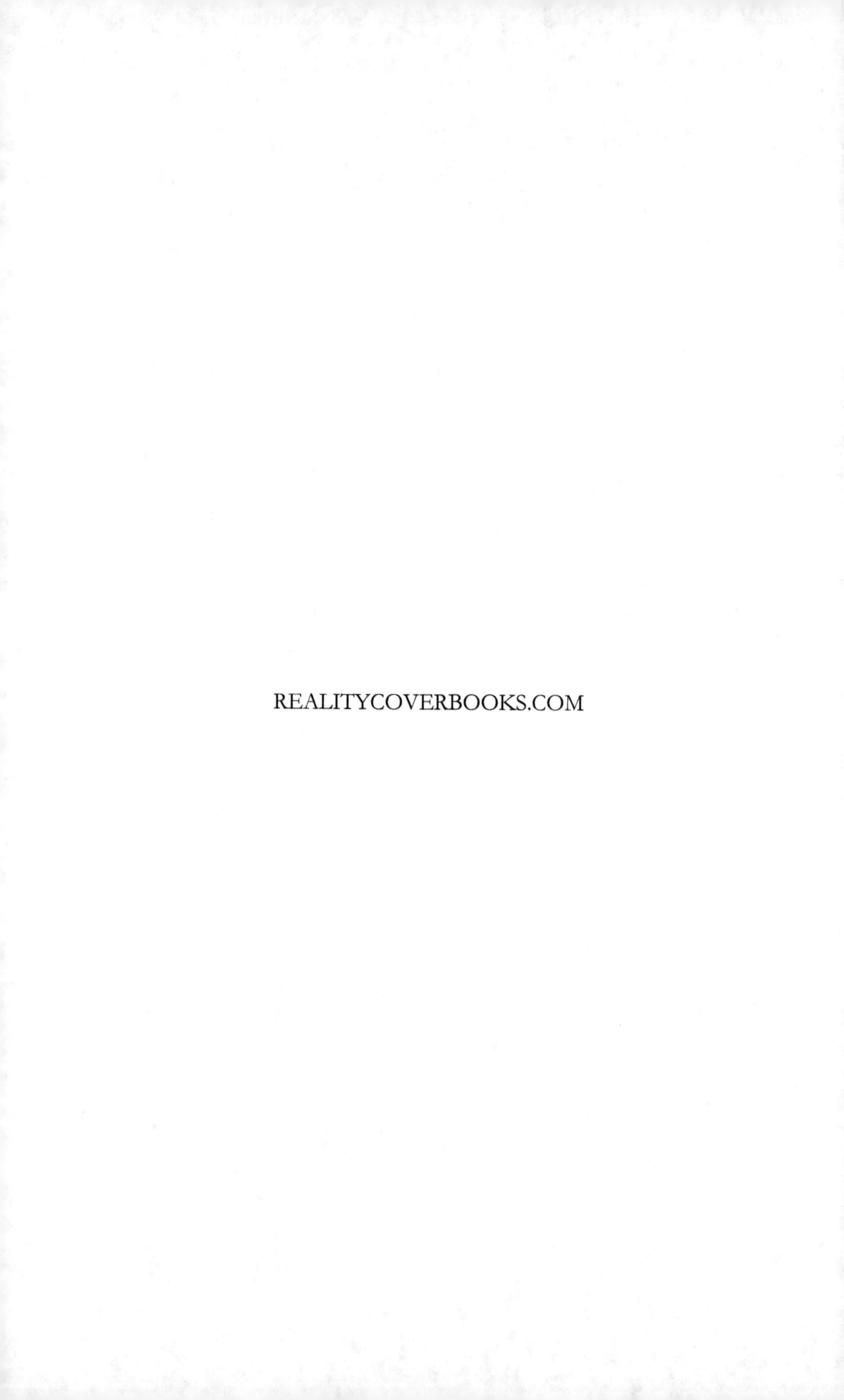
REALITYCOVERBOOKS.COM

www.ingramcontent.com/pod-product-compliance
Lightning Source LLC
Chambersburg PA
CBHW050912260726
48660CB00001B/155